A Royal Night

FOREWORD

I was in Stratford-upon-Avon composing for an RSC production when I got a call from director Julian Jarrold, with whom I'd previously worked on a dramatization of the *Great Train Robbery*.

For that score we employed elements of 60s' Jazz, which infused the score and rooted the piece in that period. The project Julian was now calling about was also to have Jazz laced through the score, but this time from the 1940s. Specifically, 1945, as shooting was about to begin for *A Royal Night Out*.

The film would fictionalize and embellish a true event: that of the young Princess Elizabeth, our future Queen, and her sister Princess Margaret leaving Buckingham Palace on VE night, to witness the celebrations in the streets of London. It sounded to me like a wonderful job for a composer, the script calling for period swing music, as well as delicate, intimate scoring for Elizabeth's internal hopes and fears for her future role as Monarch, and bubbly, capricious, jazz for stretches of the film where the Royal sisters become separated and find themselves in various scrapes.

Julian shot the movie with his usual visual flair and beauty, and I was able to contribute ideas throughout the edit, which is always a benefit to me when it comes to final scoring. We were lucky enough to record the Orchestra and Big Band at Galaxy Studio, near Brussels; a state of the art facility in the Belgium countryside, employing some of Europe's finest musicians.

I then wrote the 'source' type music, which appears in the film coming from inside nightclubs, barracks, from parties or dances. This gave me a chance to write some catchy jazz tunes independent from the themes of the score. We recorded these at Kenilworth Studios in London, with a band of brilliant session jazz players.

I owe a huge debt of thanks to a fantastic team for making the process smooth and, most importantly, great fun.

Paul Englishby

Published by
Wise Publications
14-15 Berners Street, London W1T 3LJ, UK.

Exclusive Distributors:
Music Sales Limited
Distribution Centre, Newmarket Road,
Bury St Edmunds, Suffolk IP33 3YB, UK.
Music Sales Pty Limited
4th floor, Lisgar House, 30-32 Carrington Street,
Sydney, NSW 2000, Australia.

Order No. AM1010933
ISBN: 978-1-78558-040-6
This book © Copyright 2015 Wise Publications,
a division of Music Sales Limited.

Edited by Jenni Norey.
Music arranged by Alistair Watson.
Music processed by Paul Ewers Music Design.
Original CD Cover design by WLP Ltd.
With thanks to Paul Englishby.

Printed in the EU.

Your Guarantee of Quality:

As publishers, we strive to produce every book
to the highest commercial standards.

This book has been carefully designed to minimise awkward
page turns and to make playing from it a real pleasure.
Particular care has been given to specifying acid-free, neutral-sized paper
made from pulps which have not been elemental chlorine bleached.
This pulp is from farmed sustainable forests and
was produced with special regard for the environment.

Throughout, the printing and binding have been planned to ensure
a sturdy, attractive publication which should give years of enjoyment.
If your copy fails to meet our high standards, please inform us
and we will gladly replace it.

www.musicsales.com

PRINCESS ELIZABETH (OPENING TITLES)

Music by Paul Englishby

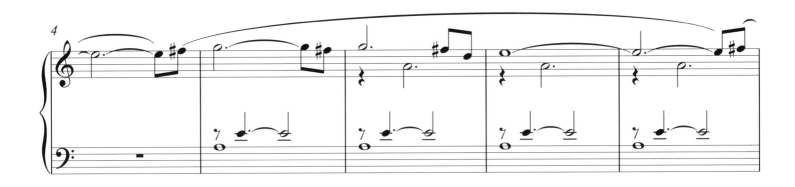

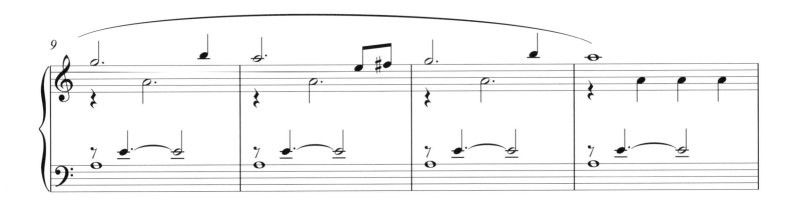

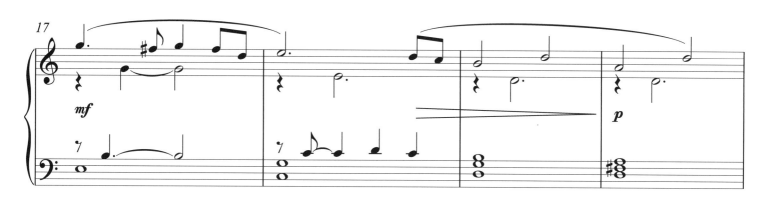

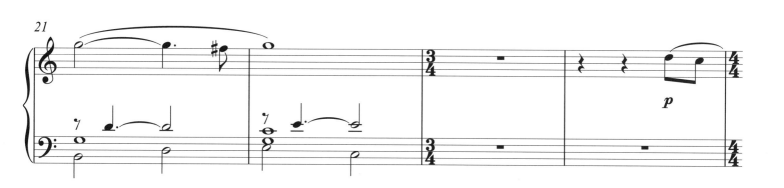

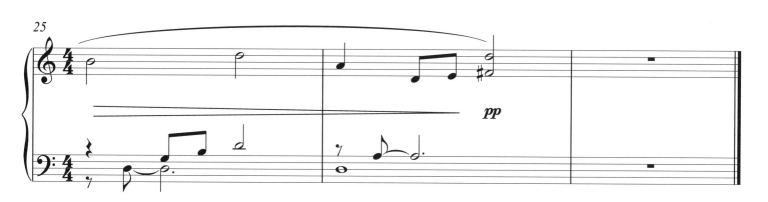

ELIZABETH ASKS

Music by Paul Englishby

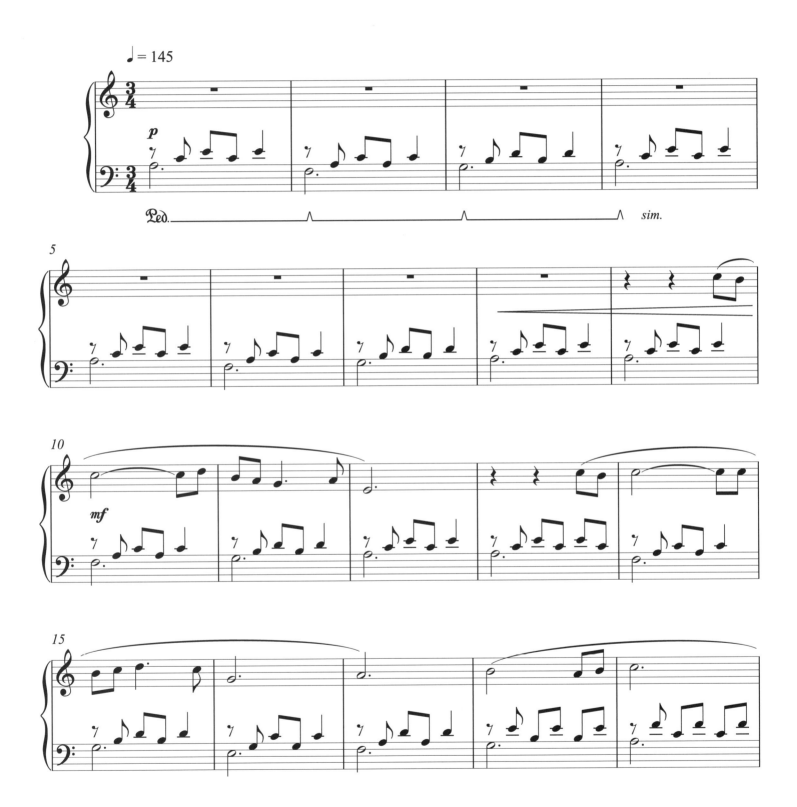

YIPPEE!

Music by Paul Englishby

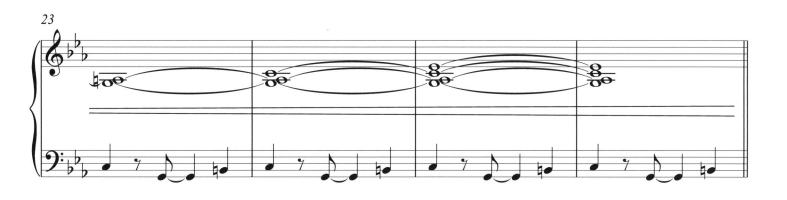

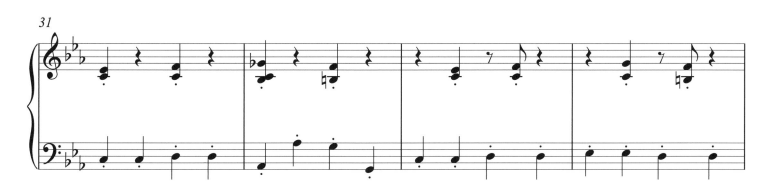

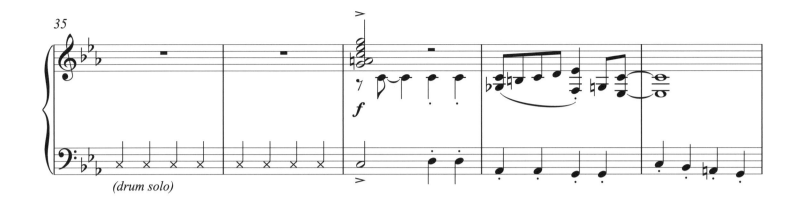

(drum solo)

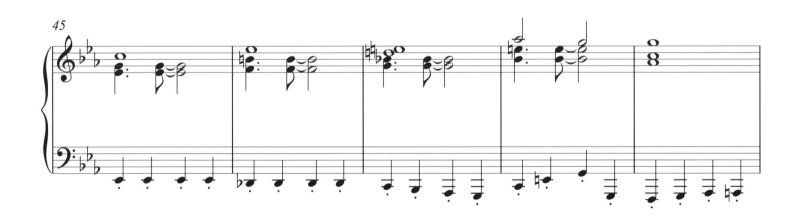

CHASING MARGARET

Music by Paul Englishby

TRAFALGAR SQUARE

Music by Paul Englishby

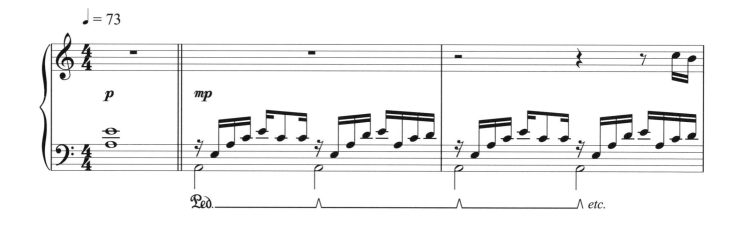

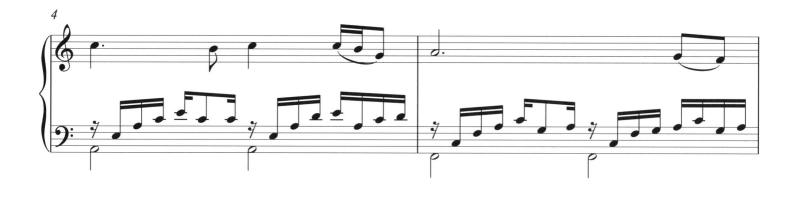

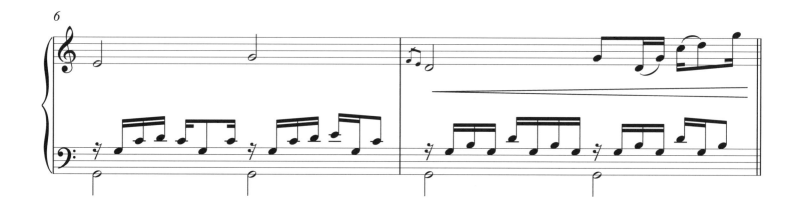

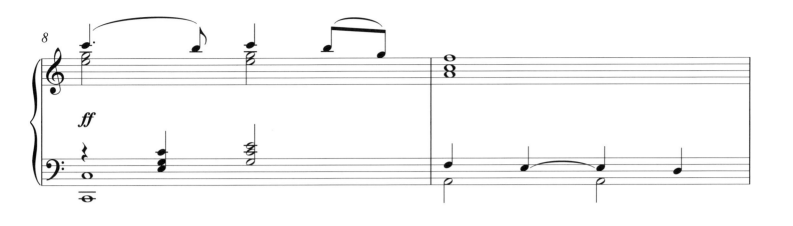

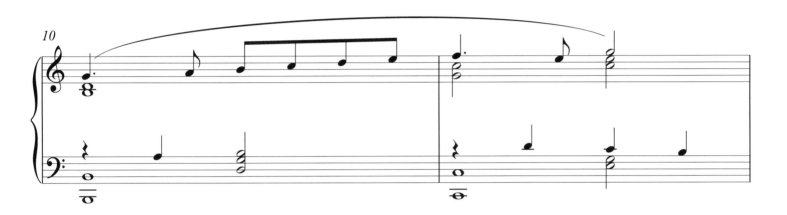

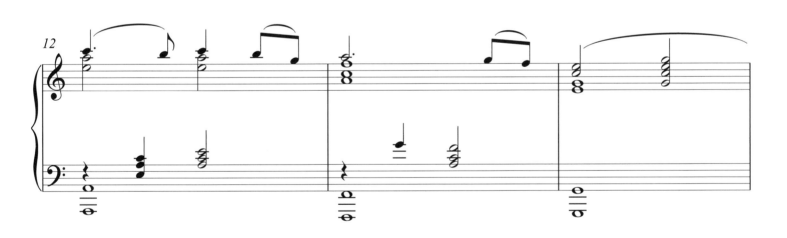

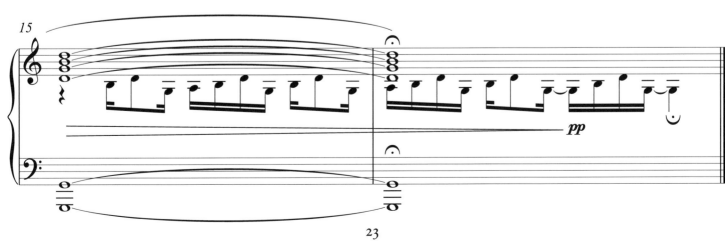

OUTSIDE THE PALACE

Music by Paul Englishby

MARGARET GOES TO CHELSEA

Music by Paul Englishby

NEW WORLD

Music by Paul Englishby

DANCE AT STAN'S

Music by Paul Englishby

TUGBOAT

Music by Paul Englishby

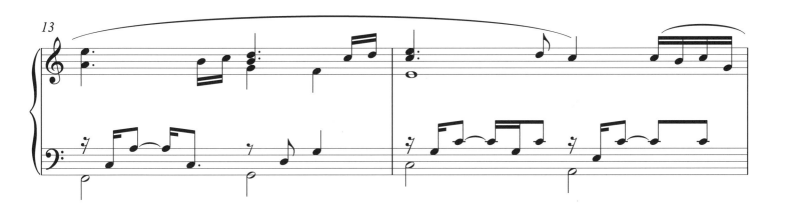

TUXEDO JUNCTION

Music by Buddy Feyne, Erskine Hawkins,
William Johnson & Julian Dash

AMERICAN PATROL

Music by F.W. Meacham

ASK YOU

Music by Paul Englishby

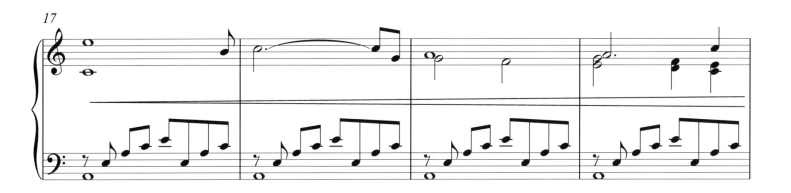

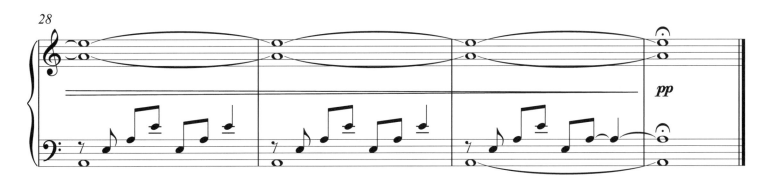

CAFÉ IN PARIS

Music by Paul Englishby

THANKS FOR EVERYTHING

Music by Paul Englishby

IN THE MOOD

Music by Joe Garland

D.S. al Coda

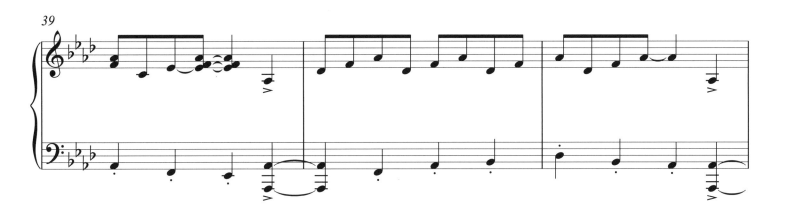

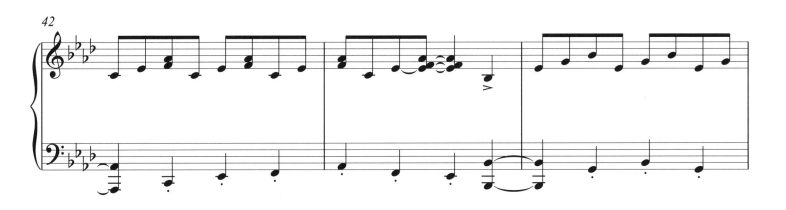

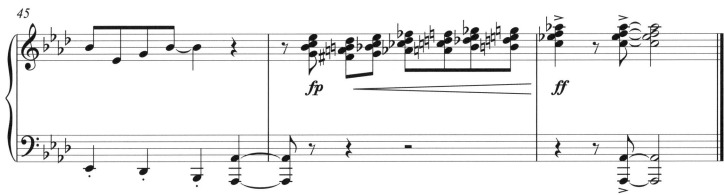

THINGS AIN'T
WHAT THEY USED TO BE

Music by Mercer Kennedy Ellington

To Coda ⊕

Whatever you want...

Music Sales publishes the very best in printed music for rock & pop, film music, jazz, blues, country and classical as well as songs from all the great stage musicals.

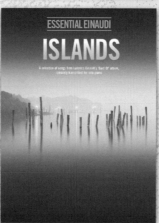

Many of our practical publications come with helpful CDs or exclusive download links to music files for backing tracks and other audio extras.

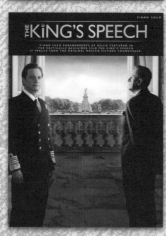

We also publish a range of tuition titles, books for audition use and book+DVD master classes that let you learn from the world's greatest performers.

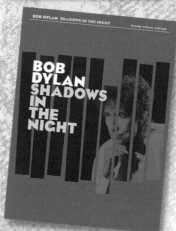

So, whatever you want, Music Sales has it.

Just visit your local music shop and ask to see our huge range of music in print.

In case of difficulty, contact marketing@musicsales.co.uk